still ht

's chain ha

ry brings t

ys around m

Fond Memory

In fond memory of our parents:
Pilib Ó Laoghaire and Eileen Donovan,
Con McCarthy and Agnes O'Connor.

Fond Memory

CONSOLING WORDS FROM
THE IRISH TRADITION

Edited by Íde Ní Laoghaire and Mary Webb

THE O'BRIEN PRESS
DUBLIN

First published 2005 by The O'Brien Press Ltd,
20 Victoria Road, Rathgar, Dublin 6, Ireland.
Tel: +353 1 4923333; Fax: +353 1 4922777
E-mail: books@obrien.ie
Website: www.obrien.ie

ISBN 0-86278-926-5

British Library Cataloguing-in-Publication Data
Fond memory : consoling words from the Irish tradition
1.Consolation - Quotations, maxims, etc. 2.Prayers 3.Quotations, Irish
4.Ireland - Quotations, maxims, etc.
I.Ní Laoghaire, Íde II.Webb, Mary
242.4

1 2 3 4 5 6 7 8 9 10
05 06 07 08 09 10 11

Cover painting: 'Lily White, Brick Red' © Patricia McGloughlin is reproduced by
kind permission of the artist and photographed by Silver Image Photography.

Typesetting, layout, editing, design: The O'Brien Press Ltd
Printing: Bercker, Germany

CONTENTS

Wind and wave, and moon and stars,

shall sing you lullaby …

We are holding hands for ever …

The beauty of an aged face ...

IN EXILE

I am of Ireland ...

May the road rise to meet you ...

RELIGIOUS / SPIRITUAL

Be Thou my vision …

Between God and His right hand …

PART 11 REFLECTION

Peace comes dropping slow ...

Preface

The idea for this book sprang from several sources. Firstly there was the realisation that while several collections existed which provided suggestions for readings and contemplation around the time of bereavement, there was none specific to the Irish tradition and reflecting the Irish experience. We wondered: was there a need for such a book?

Then, a friend of one of us called from London to ask if we could suggest something she might read at her father's funeral which would capture his Irish background. She particularly wanted to include something in the Irish language, something short and simple which she could actually say, as her own Irish was virtually non-existent.

Times of loss and bereavement often leave us unable to say what we really feel — either about our own emotions and grief, or about the loved one we have lost. Yet this is the very time when it seems most important that the words are right, that something very tangible of the character and spirit of the person who has gone be conveyed to those who are gathered to mourn and remember. We want what is said to be worthy of them.

In this collection you will find poems, sayings, songs and prayers that celebrate and remember the lives of parents, partners, children, loved ones old and young, whom

13

we miss and for whom we grieve; there is a poem for a musician, words to remember a countryman, recollections of good friends and companions. Although we have included the full text of most poems, it may be that just a few lines, or even one line, will encapsulate the person: 'And O she was the Sunday / in every week'; 'You were a part of the green country'. For ease of reference, poems have been grouped under categories, but they may be relevant under a number of headings.

Bearing in mind the huge numbers of Irish people who form part of the diaspora, and how important it is for them to be re-connected to their homeland and heritage, we have devoted a section, In Exile, especially to pieces that express the emigrant's love for their native place, for example, the song 'Galway Bay'. We have included some of the favourite poems that have travelled with emigrants, or those that capture the childhood of the generation now in their later years.

We also wanted to include more modern voices and have searched for pieces we felt were in tune with the aim of the book.

We have been very selective in the collection, opting for those poets who tend to work with the moods appropriate to the purpose of the book and often choosing several from a particular writer rather than attempting to make this collection representative of the body of Irish writing. We sneaked in the writers Newman and Hopkins, both of whom spent time living and working in Ireland, because their work has become part of the familiar.

As well as choices made for their power and expressive qualities as public readings, there are poems for quiet personal reflection, poems to comfort and console, to prompt memory, to give support in the times before and after funeral ceremonies, or to offer hope for going forward.

PART I

Readings

LOVED ONES

*God made my mother
on an April day ...*

My Mother
Francis Ledwidge

God made my mother on an April day,
From sorrow and the mist along the sea,
Lost birds' and wanderers' songs and ocean spray,
And the moon loved her wandering jealously.

Beside the ocean's din she combed her hair,
Singing the nocturne of the passing ships,
Before her earthly lover found her there
And kissed away the music from her lips.

She came unto the hills and saw the change
That brings the swallow and the geese in turns.
But there was not a grief she deemed strange,
For there is that in her which always mourns.

Kind heart she has for all on hill or wave
Whose hopes grew wings like ants to fly away.
I bless the God Who such a mother gave
This poor bird-hearted singer of a day.

Mother
Enda Wyley

There is a room in my head, to which you often
  come,
orchid gifts wet with rain in one hand —
in the other, your love
wrapped up in a cut-out newspaper piece
you'd saved just for me
or maybe sealed tight in irregular pots
of home-made orange jam.

You come in and we quickly leave behind
the thorny rose-gardens of our grown-up fights.
I smooth out the creases in your gentle face
I know I've often caused —
while you, keeping me from the shabby coldness
of this outside world,
put the last stitch on my coat.

In Memory of My Mother
Patrick Kavanagh

I do not think of you lying in the wet clay
Of a Monaghan graveyard; I see
You walking down a lane among the poplars
On your way to the station, or happily

Going to second Mass on a summer Sunday –
You meet me and you say:
'Don't forget to see about the cattle –'
Among your earthiest words the angels stray.

And I think of you walking along a headland
Of green oats in June,
So full of repose, so rich with life –
And I see us meeting at the end of a town

On a fair day by accident, after
The bargains are all made and we can walk
Together through the shops and stalls and markets
Free in the oriental streets of thought.

O you are not lying in the wet clay,
For it is a harvest evening now and we
Are piling up the ricks against the moonlight
And you smile up at us – eternally.

Any Woman
Katharine Tynan

I am the pillars of the house;
The keystone of the arch am I.
Take me away, and roof and wall
Would fall to ruin utterly.

I am the fire upon the hearth,
I am the light of the good sun,
I am the heat that warms the earth,
Which else were colder than a stone.

At me the children warm their hands;
I am their light of love alive.
Without me cold the hearthstone stands,
Nor could the precious children thrive.

I am the twist that holds together
The children in its sacred ring,
Their knot of love, from whose close tether
No lost child goes a-wandering.

I am the house from floor to roof,
I deck the walls, the board I spread;
I spin the curtains, warp and woof,
And shake the down to be their bed.

I am their wall against all danger,
Their door against the wind and snow,
Thou Whom a woman laid in manger,
Take me not till the children grow!

Caesura
Áine Miller

An adverbial clause,
the when
of her going
hangs on my days.

I pause
between visits,
to find grammar in our love,
a compound of prepositions, the list

she made me rhyme
when I came to her for a start
in my Composition, or
to have spellings heard,

trips off my tongue easily
as the years:
about above according to, across after against,
along amid amidst among amongst around,
at before behind below beneath between

betwixt, by concerning during excepting for
from into ...

at into falters ... still
no mistress of what comes after,
to govern relationship,
define an absence.

I want nothing
other than the common
noun she makes proper, Mother,
and wordless pause before I stumble on

without

Mother
D L Kelleher

I have lost her, I know;
But she is with me still, wherever I go,
        In thought or in dream,
        Like the gleam
Of a silvery evening shut in a little pool
That a child sees, and he coming from school
With a primrose in his hand,
        And he swinging it left and right
In a way you would never understand,
        Unless you could see with that other sight

The skilled musicians there,
Around him in the nimble air.

A Summer Day
Robert Greacen

Dream of a summer day: a hearse,
Bleached tombstones, gold letters glinting.
A stone forest in a city suburb.
Beloved husband, much-loved son,
Thy will, O Lord, not ours be done.
Mother in the oak coffin; yes, at last
After much pain and long, hard years
That came to nearly eighty-eight.
Voiceless I stand, her often wayward boy,
While the minister intones grave words
I hear but don't quite grasp:
'Receive Elizabeth, Thy servant here.'
Sweetest of names, Elizabeth,
Each syllable a childhood bell.
Dismay and guilt in this neat wilderness,
I don't know where to turn my head.
Down, down, down. Wood unto earth.
Gravediggers tipped. All smoothly done.
Back now to the shining city
And the Victorians round the City Hall
Frozen for ever in their sooty marble.
Gone, gone, gone, gone. All gone.

Back from the rectangles of the quiet dead.
Back to memory and guilt. Back to dismay.
Back to the nightmare of a summer day.

The Recipe
Jean O'Brien

Every Christmas I take out her old book,
its leaves browned, the paper
dried to tissue. Carefully I turn the pages
and smile at recipes for invalids —
beef tea, real lemonade —
until I get to the cakes
where her hand jotted on the margins
her own preferred mix of raisins, sultanas,
orange peel and cherries. The ink
vanishes into the crumbling edge.

I still have her baking tin
greased up to hold off the rust.
I weigh and sift her every word
looking for some meaning
in the method. All I find are weights
and measures doled out in pounds
and ounces, the only recipe
I ever took from her.
I am still uneasy till it rises.

I will go with my father a-ploughing ...

I Will Go With My Father a-Ploughing
Joseph Campbell

I will go with my father a-ploughing
To the green field by the sea,
And the rooks and the crows and the seagulls
Will come flocking after me.
I will sing to the patient horses
With the lark in the white of the air,
And my father will sing the plough-song
That blesses the cleaving share.

I will go with my father a-sowing
To the red field by the sea,
And the rooks and the gulls and the starlings
Will come flocking after me.
I will sing to the striding sowers
With the finch on the flowering sloe,
And my father will sing the seed-song
That only the wise men know.

I will go with my father a-reaping
To the brown field by the sea,
And the geese and the crows and the children
Will come flocking after me.
I will sing to the weary reapers
With the wren in the heat of the sun,
And my father will sing the scythe-song
That joys for the harvest done.

Father and Son
F R Higgins

Only last week, walking the hushed fields
Of our most lovely Meath, now thinned by
    November,
I came to where the road from Laracor leads
To the Boyne river — that seemed more lake than
    river,
Stretched in uneasy light and stript of reeds.

And walking longside an old weir
Of my people's, where nothing stirs — only the
    shadowed
Leaden flight of a heron up the lean air —
I went unmanly with grief, knowing how my father,
Happy though captive in years, walked last with me
    there.

Yes, happy in Meath with me for a day
He walked, taking stock of herds hid in their own
    breathing;
And naming colts, gusty as wind, once steered by
    his hand,
Lightnings winked in the eyes that were half shy in
    greeting
Old friends — the wild blades, when he gallivanted
    the land.

For that proud, wayward man now my heart breaks —
Breaks for that man whose mind was a secret eyrie,
Whose kind hand was sole signet of his race,
Who curbed me, scorned my green ways, yet
    increasingly loved me
Till Death drew its grey blind down his face.

And yet I am pleased that even my reckless ways
Are living shades of his rich calms and passions —
Witnesses for him and for those faint namesakes
With whom now he is one, under yew branches,
Yes, one in a graven silence no bird breaks.

Going Home to Mayo, Winter, 1949
Paul Durcan

Leaving behind us the alien, foreign city of Dublin
My father drove through the night in an old Ford
    Anglia,
His five-year-old son in the seat beside him,
The rexine seat of red leatherette,
And a yellow moon peered in through the wind-
    screen.
'Daddy, Daddy,' I cried, 'Pass out the moon,'
But no matter how hard he drove he could not
    pass out the moon.
Each town we passed through was another milestone
And their names were magic passwords into eternity:
Kilcock, Kinnegad, Strokestown, Elphin,
Tarmonbarry, Tulsk, Ballaghaderreen, Ballavarry;
Now we were in Mayo and the next stop was
    Turlough,
The village of Turlough in the heartland of Mayo,
And my father's mother's house, all oil-lamps and
    women,
And my bedroom over the public bar below,
And in the morning cattle-cries and cock-crows:
Life's seemingly seamless garment gorgeously rent
By their screeches and bellowings. And in the
    evenings
I walked with my father in the high grass down by
    the river

Talking with him — an unheard-of thing in the city.
But home was not home and the moon could be
  no more outflanked
Than the daylight nightmare of Dublin city:
Back down along the canal we chugged into the city
And each lock-gate tolled our mutual doom;
And railings and palings and asphalt and traffic-
  lights,
And blocks after blocks of so-called 'new'
  tenements —
Thousands of crosses of loneliness planted
In the narrowing grave of the life of the father;
In the wide, wide cemetery of the boy's childhood.

Father and Son
Robert Greacen

I can't remember how it happened,
How hatred seeded and grew rank,
A tall weed that dwarfed us both
And flourished till it stank.

Yet that isn't the whole story.
I remember evenings when, father and son,
We walked the velvety spring streets
And greeted the blossoms one by one.

Images became blurred, then clear
To harshness, violence; but still
Behind the bitter word, the angry gesture,
I find the love that neither wished to kill.

Rest in peace, my father, trespass forgiven,
The dark stains whitened out. Today
The siren screams our armistice,
The angry dwarfs ride fast away.

The Return
Katharine Tynan

I rested in your easy chair,
Slept in your late-abandoned bed
And felt your pleasure everywhere,
A benediction on my head,
Through sleep and waking: all the while
I was quite sure I felt your smile.

I knelt and laid my cheek upon
The cushions that you lately pressed;
All your familiar things forgone
Took to my own use and behest,
Quite sure your spirit leant to bless
Your daughter in that loneliness.

I sat beside your fire aglow,
In the dim hours 'twixt night and day,
And knew you would be glad to know,
You who gave everything away –
I had your old room, sweet and warm,
Safe from the winter night and storm.

I slept, I rose, I rested there;
My thoughts, my dreams were still and glad.
The dear room kept its happy air
As in the golden years we had;
And sleeping, waking, all the while
I was quite sure I felt your smile.

Wind and wave,
and moon and stars,
shall sing you lullaby ...

A Rathlin Cradle Song
John Irvine

The night is on the dark sea wave
And the boats are on the deep,
But here within the quiet room
My treasure lies asleep.
Oh! may Our Lady come and bless
The cradle where you lie,
And wind and wave, and moon and stars,
Shall sing you lullaby.

The woodland birds are silent now,
And the empty fields are still.
Night in her sable vestment walks
Across the lonely hill.
Oh! may Our Lady stoop to rock
The cradle where you lie,
And wind and wave, and moon and stars,
Shall sing you lullaby.

A Little Boy in the Morning
Francis Ledwidge

He will not come, and still I wait.
He whistles at another gate
Where angels listen. Ah, I know
He will not come, yet if I go
How shall I know he did not pass
Barefooted in the flowery grass?

The moon leans on one silver horn
Above the silhouettes of morn,
And from their nest-sills finches whistle
Or stooping pluck the downy thistle.
How is the morn so gay and fair
Without his whistling in the air?

The world is calling, I must go.
How shall I know he did not pass
Barefooted in the shining grass?

Tree of Life
Eavan Boland

A tree on a moonless night
has no sap or colour.

It has no flower and no fruit.
It waits for the sun to find them.
I cannot find you
in this dark hour
dear child

wait
for dawn
to make us clear to one another.

Let the sun
inch above the rooftops.

Let love be the light that shows again
the blossom to the root.

A Cradle Song
Padraic Colum

O men from the fields!
Come gently within.
Tread softly, softly,
O men coming in.

Mavourneen is going
From me and from you,
Where Mary will fold him
With mantle of blue!

From reek of the smoke
And cold of the floor,
And the peering of things
Across the half-door.

O men from the fields!
Soft, softly come thro'.
Mary puts round him
Her mantle of blue.

Babes Who Died
Eithne Strong

I do not know where they have gone
my two who went out into the night.
I do not know where I can find them
these two who have gone in the dark
I
so aching out
so numb and cold
in the voiceless night.

Golden Stockings
Oliver St John Gogarty

Golden stockings you had on
In the meadow where you ran;
And your little knees together
Bobbed like pippins in the weather
When the breezes rush and fight
For those dimples of delight;
And they dance from the pursuit,
And the leaf looks like the fruit.

I have many a sight in mind
That would last if I were blind;
Many verses I could write
That would bring me many a sight.
Now I only see but one,
See you running in the sun;
And the gold-dust coming up
From the trampled butter-cup.

Gravechild, Renvyle
Eamon Grennan

Day dries shining
Like laundered sheets.
In the ruined churchyard the grass
Takes the broken stones
To heart, like hurt children.

A small cross stands to the memory
Of Noreen daughter of Fanny Wade
Five in October 1908.
Faintly the stone proclaims
Jesus called a little girl.

Through cracks in the old wall,
Maidenhair celandine star-moss
Recall Fanny's only daughter.
Redbreast and chittering wren
Sweeten her breath in brambles.

March, and she's a girl again:
Springtides rise in her veins, her
Open arms candid with daffodils,
Where she runs to rouse her drowsy mother,
Expectant in her grassgreen bed.

Elegy for a Child
Paula Meehan

It is not that the spring brings
You back. Birds riotous about
The house, fledglings learn to fly.

Nor that coming on petals drifted in the orchard
Is like opening your door, a draught of pastel,
A magpie hoard of useless bright.

Clouds move over the river
Under the sun — a cotton sheet shook out.
The pines bring me news
From deeper in the woods:
The rain will come sing on the roof soon.

It is not the day's work in the garden,
The seedlings neatly leaf mould mulched in lines.
Not the woodpile trim bespeaking good husbandry
And conjuring up the might-have-been.

It is not the anarchic stream
In a stone sucking dash past the crane's haunt, fickle,
Sky mirror now, now shattered bauble,

Nor the knowledge of planets in proper orbit,
Their passage through my fourth house
Fixed before I was born.

It is not that the night you died
A star plummeted to earth.
It is not that I watched it fall.

It is not that I was your mother,
Nor the rooted deep down loss,
That has brought me to this moment
To sit by the window and weep.

You were but a small bird ready
Within me, balanced for flight.

Prayer for a Little Child
Winifred Letts

God keep my jewel this day from danger;
From tinker and pooka and black-hearted stranger.
From harm of the water, from hurt of the fire.
From the horns of the cows going home to the byre.
From the sight of the fairies that maybe might
   change her.
From teasing the ass when he's tied to the manger.
From stones that would bruise her, from thorns of
   the briar.
From red evil berries that wake her desire.
From hunting the gander and vexing the goat.
From the depths o' sea water by Danny's old boat.

From cut and from tumble, from sickness and
   weeping;
May God have my jewel this day in his keeping.

Mid-Term Break
Seamus Heaney

I sat all morning in the college sick bay,
Counting bells knelling classes to a close.
At two o'clock our neighbours drove me home.

In the porch I met my father crying —
He had always taken funerals in his stride —
And Big Jim Evans saying it was a hard blow.

The baby cooed and laughed and rocked the pram
When I came in, and I was embarrassed
By old men standing up to shake my hand

And tell me they were 'sorry for my trouble'.
Whispers informed strangers I was the eldest,
Away at school, as my mother held my hand

In hers and coughed out angry tearless sighs.
At ten o'clock the ambulance arrived
With the corpse, stanched and bandaged by the
   nurses.

Next morning I went up into the room. Snow-
  drops
And candles soothed the bedside; I saw him
For the first time in six weeks. Paler now,

Wearing a poppy bruise on his left temple,
He lay in the four foot box as in his cot.
No gaudy scars, the bumper knocked him clear.

A four foot box, a foot for every year.

The Grey Dusk
Seumas O'Sullivan

Tremulous grey of dusk,
Deepening into the blue,
It is the path that leads
Ever to you.

Child of the dusk, your eyes
Quietly light my way,
Quiet as evening stars,
Quiet and grey.

All the magic of dusk,
Tremulous, grey and blue,
Gathers into my heart,
Quiet for you.

Spring and Fall:
[to a young child]
Gerard Manley Hopkins

Margaret, are you grieving
Over Goldengrove unleaving?
Leaves, like the things of man, you
With your fresh thoughts care for, can you?
Ah! as the heart grows older
It will come to such sights colder
By and by, nor spare a sigh,
Though worlds of wanwood leafmeal lie;
And yet you *will* weep and know why.
Now no matter, child, the name:
Sorrow's springs are the same.
Nor mouth had, no nor mind, expressed
What heart heard of, ghost guessed:
It is the blight man was born for,
It is Margaret you mourn for.

All-Souls
Katharine Tynan

The door of Heaven is on the latch
To-night, and many a one is fain
To go home for one's night's watch
With his love again.

Oh, where the father and mother sit
There's a drift of dead leaves at the door
Like pitter-patter of little feet
That come no more.

Their thoughts are in the night and cold,
Their tears are heavier than the clay,
But who is this at the threshold
So young and gay?

They are come from the land o' the young,
They have forgotten how to weep;
Words of comfort on the tongue,
And a kiss to keep.

They sit down and they stay awhile,
Kisses and comfort none shall lack;
At morn they steal forth with a smile
And a long look back.

Boys
Winifred Letts

I do be thinking God must laugh
The time He makes a boy;
All element the creatures are,
And divilmint and joy.
Careless and gay as a wad in a window,

Swift as a redshank, and wild as a hare;
Heartscalds and torments — but sorra a mother
Has got one to spare.

Beech Tree
Patrick Kavanagh

I planted in February
A bronze-leafed beech,
In the chill brown soil
I spread out its silver fibres.

Protected it from the goats
With wire-netting
And fixed it firm against
The worrying wind.

Now it is safe, I said,
April must stir
My precious baby
To greenful loveliness.

It is August now, I have hoped
But I hope no more —
My beech tree will never hide sparrows
From hungry hawks.

Child Burial
Paula Meehan

Your coffin looked unreal,
fancy as a wedding cake.

I chose your grave clothes with care,
your favourite stripey shirt,

your blue cotton trousers.
They smelt of woodsmoke, of October,

your own smell there too.
I chose a gansy of homespun wool,

warm and fleecy for you. It is
so cold down in the dark.

No light can reach you and teach you
the paths of wild birds,

the names of the flowers,
the fishes, the creatures.

Ignorant you must remain
of the sun and its work,

my lamb, my calf, my eaglet,
my cub, my kid, my nestling,

my suckling, my colt. I would spin
time back, take you again

within my womb, your amniotic lair,
and further spin you back

through nine waxing months
to the split seeding moment

you chose to be made flesh,
word within me.

I'd cancel the love feast
the hot night of your making.

I would travel alone
to a quiet mossy place,

you would spill from me into the earth
drop by bright red drop.

We are holding hands
for ever ...

Sacrament
John F Deane

You, pictured for ever, before me;
I stand in black and wear a white
carnation; you, holding an array
of golden roses, maidenhair, smile up
at me and you are beautiful; your body
washed for me and gently scented;
you, set apart in white, a mystery,
all sacred:
　　　　we are holding hands for ever,
dedicated; such are the signs of a deep
　abiding grace.

　　　　Another image
graven on my mind; you lie, again
in white; on your breast a silken
picture of the Virgin; they have washed
your body, closed your eyes, you hold
no flowers; vein-blue traces
of suffering on your skin, your fingers

locked together, away from me.

But it is I who have loved you, known
the deepest secrets of your grace; I take
the golden ring from your finger; I kiss
the bride,

And they close the heavy doors
against me, of that silent, vast cathedral.

O Do Not Love Too Long
W B Yeats

[Verse 2]
All through the years of our youth
Neither could have known
Their own thought from the other's
We were so much at one.

The Patriot's Wife
Charles Gavan Duffy

[Last verse]
For still to me, dear friend, dear love,
Or both — dear wife,
Your image comes with serious thoughts,
But tender, rife;
No idle plaything to caress or chide
In sport or strife,

But my best chosen friend, companion, guide,
To walk through life,
Linked hand-in-hand, two equal, loving friends,
true husband and true wife.

Mo Ghile Mear
Traditional

Seal da rabhas im' mhaighdean shéimh,
'S anois im' bhaintreach chaite thréith,
Mo chéile ag treabhadh na dtonn go tréan
De bharr na gcnoc is i n-imigcéin.

[Curfá:]
'Sé mo laoch, mo Ghile Mear,
'Sé mo Chaesar, Ghile Mear,
Suan ná séan ní bhfuaireas féin
Ó chuaigh i gcéin mo Ghile Mear.

Ní labhrann cuach go suairc ar nóin
Is níl guth gadhair i gcoillte cnó,
Ná maidin shamhraidh i gcleanntaibh ceoigh
Ó d'imthigh uaim an buachaill beó.
[Curfá]

Marcach uasal uaibhreach óg,
Gas gan gruaim is suairce snódh,

Glac is luaimneach, luath i ngleo
Ag teascadh an tslua 's ag tuargain treon.
[Curfá]

Seinntear stair ar chlairsigh cheoil
's líontair táinte cárt ar bord
Le hinntinn ard gan chaim, gan cheó
Chun saoghal is sláinte d' fhagháil dom leómhan.
[Curfá]

Ghile Mear 'sa seal faoi chumha,
's Éire go léir faoi chlócaibh dubha;
Suan ná séan ní bhfuaireas féin
Ó luaidh i gcéin mo Ghile Mear.
[Curfá]

Translation: My Dashing Darling

For a while I was a gentle maiden
And now a spent worn-out widow
My spouse ploughing the waves strongly
Over the hills and far away.

[Chorus:]
He is my hero, my dashing darling
He is my Caesar, dashing darling.
I've had no rest from forebodings
Since he went far away, my darling.

The cuckoo sings not pleasantly at noon
And the sound of hounds is not heard in nut
    woods,
Nor summer morning in misty glen
Since he went away from me, my lively boy.
[Chorus]

Noble, proud young horseman
Warrior unsaddened, of most pleasant countenace
A swift-moving hand, quick in a fight,
Slaying the enemy and smiting the strong.
[Chorus]

Let a strain be played on musical harps
And let many quarts be filled
With high spirit without fault or mist
For life and health to toast my lion.
[Chorus]

Dashing darling, for a while under sorrow
And all Ireland under black cloaks
Rest or pleasure I did not get
Since he went far away, my dashing darling.
[Chorus]

Any Wife
Katharine Tynan

[Verse 1]
Nobody knows but you and I, my dear,
And the stars, the spies of God, that lean and
  peer,
Those nights when you and I in a narrow strait
Were under the whips of God and desolate.
In extreme pain, in uttermost agony,
We bore the cross for each other, you and I,
When through the darkest hour, the night of
  dread,
I suffered and you supported my head.

A Visit from My Wife
Jeremiah O'Donovan Rossa

A single glance, and that glance the first,
And her image was fixed in my mind and nursed;
And now it is woven with all my schemes,
And it rules the realm of all my dreams.

One of Heaven's best gifts in an earthly mould,
With a figure Appelles might paint of old —
All a maiden's charms with a matron's grace,
And the blossom and bloom off the peach in
  her face.

And the genius that flashes her bright black eye
Is the face of the sun in a clouded sky;
She has noble thoughts — she has noble aims
And these thoughts on her tongue are sparkling
  gems.

With a gifted mind and spirit meek
She would right the wronged and assist the weak;
She would scorn dangers to cheer the brave,
She would smite oppression and free the slave.

Yet a blighted life is my loved one's part,
And death's cold shroud is around her heart,
For winds from the 'clouds of fate' have blown
That force her to face the hard world alone.

And a daughter she of trampled land,
With its children exiled, prisoned, banned;
And she vowed her love to a lover whom
The tyrant had marked for a felon's doom.

And snatched from her side e'er the honeymoon
  wanted:
In the dungeons of England he lies enchained;
And the bonds that bind him 'for life' a slave
Are binding his love to his living grave.

He would sever the link of such hopeless love,
Were that sentence 'for ever' decreed above.

For the pleasures don't pay for the pains of life —
To be living in death with a widowed wife.

A single glance, and that glance the first,
And her image was fixed in my mind and nursed,
And now she's the woof of my worldly schemes,
And she sits enthroned as the queen of my
  dreams.

St Andrew's Day, 1985
Robert Greacen

St Andrew's Day, blind November fumbling
The hurt leaves, bleached gutter orphans.
Half-light domesticates raw brick.
A mediocre day, not to be remembered.
It's 2pm at Ladbroke Grove. I board a bus.
The mourners are gathering at Glengarriff.
Is it drizzling there? I hear the rain
Touchtyping an elegy on the Bay waters.
Though in her will she said 'no flowers'
Our daughter will place veronica on the coffin
Borne through the woods to the old Killeen.

Will the funeral go to plan, discreetly,
Even in the drizzle I imagine falling
On the lands of the Gael and Planter?
I say a London goodbye to a lost wife,

Remember our time of roses, promises,
The silvered sea at Ardnagashel,
Earrings of fuchsia in the hedgerows,
Hope arching like a rainbow over all.

Echo
Thomas Moore

How sweet the answer Echo makes
To music at night,
When, roused by lute or horn, she wakes,
And far away, o'er lawns and lakes,
Goes answering light!

Yet Love hath echoes truer far,
And far more sweet,
Than e'er beneath the moonlight's star,
Of horn or lute, or soft guitar,
The songs repeat.

'Tis when the sigh, in youth sincere,
And only then,—
The sigh that's breath'd for one to hear,
Is by that one, that only dear,
Breath'd back again!

A Dead Wife

Muiríoch Ó Dálaigh

Translated by Deirdre Flanagan

[Verse 2]

A fair beautiful flower
has been plucked from the delicate bent stalk
The darling of my heart has drooped
Laden branch of yonder house

[Verses 7-9]

My body has gone from my control
And has fallen to her share
A body in two parts am I
Since the fair beautiful gentle one has gone

One of my feet, one of my sides
Her countenance like the whitethorn
No one belonged more to her than to me
She was one of my eyes, one of my hands

She was one half of my body, the bright candle
   flame
Harshly have I been dealt with oh! King:
To speak of it leaves me weak
She was the very half of my soul

Lines of Leaving
Christy Brown

I am losing you again
all again
as if you were ever mine to lose.
The pain is as deep
beyond formal possession
beyond the fierce frivolity of tears.

Absurdly you came into my world
My time-wrecked world
a quiet laugh below the thunder.
Absurdly you leave it now
as always I foreknew you would.
I live on an alien joy.

Your gentleness disarmed me
wine in my desert
peace across impassable seas
path of light in my jungle.

Now uncatchable as the wind you go
beyond the wind
and there is nothing in my world
save the straw of salvation in the amber dream.
The absurdity of that vast improbable joy.
The absurdity of you gone.

My Lagan Love
Joseph Campbell

[Verse 1]
Where Lagan stream sings lullaby,
There blows a lily fair.
The twilight gleam is in her eye,
The night is on her hair.
And, like a lovesick *leanan-sidhe*,
She has my heart in thrall,
Nor life I own, nor liberty,
For love is lord of all.

To Mary
Charles Wolfe

If I had thought thou couldst have died,
I might not weep for thee;
But I forgot, when by thy side,
That thou couldst mortal be;
It never through my mind had past
The time would e'er be o'er,
And I on thee should look my last,
And thou shouldst smile no more!

[Verse 5]
I do not think, where'er thou art,
Thou hast forgotten me;

And I, perhaps, may soothe this heart
In thinking too of thee:
Yet there was round thee such a dawn
Of light ne'er seen before,
As fancy never could have drawn,
And never can restore!

Down by the Salley Gardens
W B Yeats

Down by the salley gardens my love and I did
   meet;
She passed the salley gardens with little snow-
   white feet.
She bid me take love easy, as the leaves grow on the
   tree;
But I, being young and foolish, with her would not
   agree.

In a field by the river my love and I did stand,
And on my leaning shoulder she laid her snow-
   white hand.
She bid me take life easy, as the grass grows on the
   weirs;
But I was young and foolish, and now am full of
   tears.

Valediction
Seamus Heaney

Lady with the frilled blouse
And simple tartan skirt,
Since you have left the house
Its emptiness has hurt
All thought. In your presence
Time rode easy, anchored
On a smile; but absence
Rocked love's balance, unmoored
The days. They buck and bound
Across the calendar
Pitched from the quiet sound
Of your flower-tender
Voice. Need breaks on my strand;
You've gone, I am at sea.
Until you resume command
Self is in mutiny.

Not Lost But Gone Before
Percy French

Once, only once, upon a time,
We heard the bells of faerie chime,
And through the golden nights and days
They sang their Elfin roundelays.

The world and we were in our prime
Once, only once, upon a time.

Has Fairyland for ever flown?
— The darkness falls on me alone,
For on my sweet companion's eyes
There shines the light of Paradise.
The heights of joy I cannot climb
As we did once upon a time.

Oh, loved one of the far away,
I know that we shall meet some day,
And once again walk hand in hand
Through all the realms of Fairyland.
And Heaven's own harps around us chime,
As they did — once upon a time!

To One Dead
Francis Ledwidge

A blackbird singing
On a moss-upholstered stone,
Bluebells swinging,
Shadows wildly blown,
A song in the wood,
A ship on the sea.
The song was for you
And the ship was for me.

A blackbird singing
I hear in my troubled mind,
Bluebells swinging,
I see in a distant wind.
But sorrow and silence
Are the wood's threnody,
The silence for you
And the sorrow for me.

The Soul Kisses Goodbye
Enda Wyley

I am the soul
who leaves your body
but at the door comes back
to kiss you once
then, lonely, comes back
again and again,
my grief, jagged petals falling
on the floor of your mouth
that was always mine.

Again and again, I turn
to trawl the water caves
of your mind
where your lovers
have often drowned

trying, one last time, to catch
all those thoughts
you so assuredly pouched
in your eyes now fallen
to a desperate close.

Twice, three times
I become,
where the devil of pain
tries to dig its claws,
an angel at rest
on shoulders —
a definite breeze
cooling down the heat
of your people's loss.

I Love My Love in the Morning
Gerald Griffin

I love my love in the morning,
For she like morn is fair —
Her blushing cheek, its crimson streak,
Its clouds her golden hair.
Her glance, its beam, so soft and kind;
Her tears, its dewy showers;
And her voice, the tender whispering wind
That stirs the early bowers.

I love my love in the morning,
I love my love at noon,
For she is bright as the lord of light,
Yet mild as autumn's moon;
Her beauty is my bosom's sun,
Her faith my fostering shade,
And I will love my darling one,
Till even the sun shall fade.

I love my love in the morning,
I love my love at eve;
Her smile's soft play is like the ray
That lights the western heaven;
I loved her when the sun was high,
I loved her when she rose;
But best of all when evening's sigh
Was murmuring at its close.

What Her Absence Means
Christy Brown

It means
      no madcap delight will intrude
into the calm flow of my working hours
      no ecstatic errors perplex
my literary pretensions.

It means
      there will be time enough for thought

undistracted by brown peril of eye
     and measured litany of routine deeds
undone by the ghost of a scent.

It means
     my neglect of the Sonnets will cease
and Homer come into battle once more.
     I might even find turgid old Tennyson
less of a dead loss now.

It means
     there will be whole days to spare
for things important to a man —
     like learning to live without a woman
without altogether losing one's mind.

It means
     there is no one now to read my latest poem
with veiled unhurried eyes
     putting my nerves on the feline rack
in silence sheer she-devil hell for me.

It means
     there is no silly woman to tell me
'Take it easy — life's long anyway —
don't drink too much — get plenty of sleep —'
     and other tremendous clichés.

It means
     I am less interrupted now with love.

The Song of Wandering Aengus
W B Yeats

I went out to the hazel wood,
Because a fire was in my head,
And cut and peeled a hazel wand,
And hooked a berry to a thread;
And when white moths were on the wing,
And moth-like stars were flickering out,
I dropped the berry in a stream
And caught a little silver trout.

When I had laid it on the floor
I went to blow the fire aflame,
But something rustled on the floor,
And some one called me by my name:
It had become a glimmering girl
With apple blossom in her hair
Who called me by my name and ran
And faded through the brightening air.

Though I am old with wandering
Through hollow lands and hilly lands,
I will find out where she has gone,
And kiss her lips and take her hands;
And walk among long dappled grass,
And pluck till tide and times are done
The silver apples of the moon,
The golden apples of the sun.

In Life's Young Morning
Robert Dwyer Joyce

In life's young morning I quaffed the wine
From Love's bright bowl as it sparkling came,
And it warms me ever, that draught divine,
When I think of thee, dearest, or name thy name.
The night may fall, and the winds may blow
From palace gardens or place of tombs,
Yet I dream of our Love-time long ago
Beneath the yellow laburnum blooms.

Gay was the garden, bright shone the bower,
Like a golden tent 'neath the summer skies,
The sunbeams glittered on leaf and flower,
And light of heaven seemed in your eyes;
The night may fall, and the winds may blow,
But gladness ever my heart assumes
From that wine of love quaffed long ago
Beneath the yellow laburnum blooms.

O'er vale and forest dark falls the night,
Yet my heart goes back to the sun and shine
When you stood in the glory of girlhood bright
'Neath the golden blossoms, your hand in mine;
The night may fall, the winds may blow,
And the greenwoods wither 'neath winter glooms;
Yet it lives forever, that long ago,
Beneath the yellow laburnum blooms.

Through the misty night to the eye and ear
Come the glitter of flowers and the songs of birds, —
Come thy looks of fondness to me so dear,
And thy witching smiles and thy loving words;
The night may fall and the winds may blow,
But that hour forever my soul illumes,
— Our golden Love-time long ago,
Beneath the yellow laburnum blooms.

Bheir Mé Óró
Údar anaithnid

[Curfá:]
Bheir mé óró, bhean ó
Bheir mé óró, bhean í
Bheir mé óró ó hó
'S mé tá brónach 's tú i m'dhith.
[Curfá arís]

'S Iomaí oíche fliuch is fuar
Thug mé cuairt is mé liom féin
Nó go ráinig mé san áit
Mar a raibh grá geal mo chroí.
[Curfá]

I mo chláirseach ní raibh ceol
I mo mheoraibh ní raibh brí
Nó gur luaigh tú do rún
'S fuair mé eolas ar mo dhán.
[Curfá]

Translation: I've Gone Away

[Chorus:]
I've gone away, oh dear one,
I've gone away, oh dear one,
I've gone away
I'm miserable and missing you.
[Chorus again]

Many's the cold and wet night
I went out travelling on my own
Until I reached the place
Where the love of my heart lived.
[Chorus]

There was no music in my harp
There was no strength in my fingers
Until you told me of your love
And I found my poem.
[Chorus]

The Planter's Daughter
Austin Clarke

When night stirred the sea
And the fire brought a crowd in,
They say that her beauty
Was music in mouth
And few in the candlelight
Thought her too proud,
For the house of the planter
Is known by the trees.

Men that had seen her
Drank deep and were silent,
The women were speaking
Wherever she went —
As a bell that is rung
Or a wonder told shyly,
And O she was the Sunday
In every week.

Though Lost to Sight to Memory Dear
Thomas Moore

Sweetheart, goodbye! That flut'ring sail
Is spread to waft me far from thee;
And soon, before the farthr'ing gale
My ship shall bound upon the sea.
Perchance, all des'late and forlorn,
These eyes shall miss thee many a year;
But unforgotten every charm —
Though lost to sight, to memory dear.

Sweetheart, goodbye! One last embrace!
Oh, cruel fate, two souls to sever!
Yet in this heart's most sacred place
Thou, thou alone, shalt dwell forever;
And still shall recollection trace,
In fancy's mirror, ever near,
Each smile, each tear, that form, that face —
Though lost to sight, to memory dear.

The beauty of an aged face ...

The Old Woman
Joseph Campbell

As a white candle
In a holy place,
So is the beauty
Of an aged face.

As the spent radiance
Of the winter sun,
So is a woman
With her travail done.

Her brood gone from her,
And her thoughts as still
As the waters
Under a ruined mill.

When You Are Old
W B Yeats

When you are old and grey and full of sleep,
And nodding by the fire, take down this book,
And slowly read, and dream of the soft look
Your eyes had once, and of their shadows deep;

How many loved your moments of glad grace,
And loved your beauty with love false or true,
But one man loved the pilgrim soul in you,
And loved the sorrows of your changing face;

And bending down beside the glowing bars,
Murmur, a little sadly, how Love fled
And paced upon the mountains overhead
And hid his face amid a crowd of stars.

Remembered Joy
Anonymous

Don't grieve for me, for now I'm free!
I follow the plan God laid for me.
I saw His face, I heard His call,
I took His hand and left it all …
I could not stay another day,
To love, to laugh, to work or play;
Tasks left undone must stay that way.
And if my parting has left a void,
Then fill it with remembered joy.
A friendship shared, a laugh, a kiss …
Ah yes, these things I, too, shall miss.
My life's been full, I've savoured much:
Good times, good friends, a loved-one's touch.
Perhaps my time seemed all too brief —
Don't shorten yours with undue grief.
Be not burdened with tears of sorrow,
Enjoy the sunshine of the morrow.

You were a part of the
green country ...

To the Beloved
Katharine Tynan

You were a part of the green country,
Of the grey hills and the quiet places;
They are not the same, the fields and the mountains,
Without the lost and beloved faces,
And you were a part of the sweet country.

There's a road that winds by the foot of the
  mountains
Where I run in my dreams and you come to meet me,
With your blue eyes and your cheeks' old roses,
The old fond smile that was quick to greet me.
They are not the same, the fields and the mountains.

There is something lost, there is something lonely,
The birds are singing, the streams are calling,
The sun's the same, and the wind in the meadows.
But o'er your grave are the shadows falling,
The soul is missing, and all is lonely.

It is what they said: you were part of the country,
You were never afraid of the wind and the weather,
I can hear in dreams the feet of your pony,
You and your pony coming together,
You will drive no more through the pleasant country.

You were part of the fields and mountains,
Everyone knew you, everyone loved you;
All the world was your friend and neighbour,
The women smiled and the men approved you.
They are not the same, the fields and the mountains.

I sigh no more for the pleasant places,
The longer I've lost you the more I miss you.
My heart seeks you in dreams and shadows,
In dreams I find you, in dreams I kiss you,
And wake, alas! to the lonely places.

Elegy for a Countryman
Padraic Fallon

He made no history, even
At home in one quiet townland
Where the houses, so still in thatch and lime, are lost
In the hazy stir
And murmur of all green Ireland.

He was never a speaker at meetings,
Nor, masked among Moonlighters,
Never broke walls and scattered a landlord's herd;
Nor, later, if he heeded them,
Was he one with the Gunfighters.

Why then should I think and think of you
And talk of you to strangers
When the priest of the parish forgot your name
  before
High Mass was over and your body laid
Down obscurely with your nameless fathers?

Only that in your quiet image, brother,
So many gentle wise-eyed men awake
Over lonely fields and forlorn farmhouses
And stare at me till I speak and speak
Lest my heart break.

The Country Funeral
M J MacManus

From Arigna they come —
Irish miles a full score —
From Croghan and Mohill,
From Ballinamore.

A gathering of side-cars,
Black in the street,
Slowly they move
Through the mist and the sleet.

Slowly they go
From the heel of the town,
Over the bridge
Through a bogland of brown.

Five score of cars,
Each with its load,
A dim, black file
On the white of the road.

Their talking is all
Of their cattle and care,
And him they will meet
No more at the fair.

His sayings and ways,
And the strength of his hand,
And the height of his deeds,
In the war for the land.

And the evening is grey
Ere the tale is all told,
And the tired bones lie
In the quiet mould.

To the Man After the Harrow
Patrick Kavanagh

Now leave the check-reins slack,
The seed is flying far to-day —
The seed like stars against the black
Eternity of April clay.

This seed is potent as the seed
Of knowledge in the Hebrew Book,
So drive your horses in the creed
Of God the Father as a stook.

Forget the men on Brady's hill.
Forget what Brady's boy may say
For destiny will not fulfil
Unless you let the harrow play.

Forget the worm's opinion too
Of hooves and pointed harrow-pins,
For you are driving your horses through
The mist where Genesis begins.

The friends so linked together ...

Oft, in the Stilly Night
Thomas Moore

Oft, in the stilly night,
Ere slumber's chain hath bound me,
Fond Memory brings the light
Of other days around me:
The smiles, the tears
Of boyhood's years,
The words of love then spoken;
The eyes that shone
Now dimm'd and gone,
The cheerful hearts now broken!
Thus, in the stilly night,
Ere slumber's chain hath bound me,
Sad Memory brings the light
Of other days around me.

When I remember all
The friends, so linked together,
I've seen around me fall
Like leaves in wintry weather,

I feel like one
Who treads alone
Some banquet-hall deserted,
Whose lights are fled,
Whose garlands dead,
And all but he departed!
Thus, in the stilly night,
Ere slumber's chain hath bound me,
Sad Memory brings the light
Of other days around me.

To My Best Friend
Francis Ledwidge

I love the wet-lipped wind that stirs the hedge
And kisses that bend flowers that drooped for rain,
That stirs the poppy on the sun-burned ledge
And like a swan dies singing, without pain.
The golden bees go buzzing down to stain
The lilies' frills, and the blue harebell rings,
And the sweet blackbird in the rainbow sings.

Deep in the meadows I would sing a song,
The shallow brook my tuning-fork, the birds
My masters; and the boughs they hop along
Shall mark my time: but there shall be no words
For lurking Echo's mock; an angel herds
Words that I may not know, within, for you,
Words for the faithful meet, the good and true.

The Parting Glass
Traditional

Oh all the time that e'er I spent,
I spent it in good company;
And any harm that e'er I've done,
I trust it was to none but me;
May those I've loved through all the years
Have memories now they'll e'er recall;
So fill to me the parting glass,
Goodnight, and joy be with you all.

Oh all the comrades that e'er I had,
Are sorry for my going away;
And of all the loved ones that e'er I had
Would wish me one more day to stay.
But since it falls unto my lot
That I should leave and you should not,
I'll gently rise and I'll softly call
Goodnight, and joy be with you all.

Of all the good times that e'er we shared,
I leave to you fond memory;
And for all the friendship that e'er we had
I ask you to remember me;
And when you sit and stories tell,
I'll be with you and help recall;
So fill to me the parting glass,
Goodnight, and joy be with you all.

Stopping by a Clare Graveyard After Hours
[For Pakie Russell, 1920-1977]

Michael Coady

I've walked up two miles from the pub
      through a mystical moonscape
And it could have been three what with taking
      both sides of the road,
I lean on the wall and my breathing
      is heavy and laboured
As I give you a greeting and offer you
      talk of the world.

Below in the village the men
      and the women are sleeping,
The lights are all out and the children
      away in their dreams,
The music and talk of tonight
      are gone to wherever
The tunes and the talk of all nights
      slip away on the air.

From shore to horizon the sea
      is a ravishing silver,
Awesome and innocent, untouched
      by joy or dismay;
The grass of the summer is gathered
      and tied in the haggards,
The dark brow of Moher is dreaming
      over the bay.

I'm not here to grieve for your bones
      or the earth where they're lying,
You've company round you of neighbours
      and friends from this place;
The men and the women who danced
      to your music are with you,
United you lie in the intimate
      rhythm of clay.

I know you were always a man
      with a heart for the true thing,
For a child or a saying, a woman,
      a flower or a song,
Life that came dancing through fingers
      was most of your praying
And your darkness redeemed in the shape
      and surprise of the word.

Out of all of the years and the laughter
      just let me remember
One moment of kissing I stood
      by the sea with a girl
While you were enthroned on the hill
      with the dawn at your shoulder
Gracing your music with wakening
      song of the birds.

The tiding old sea is still taking
      and giving and shaping,

Gentians and violets break
        in the spring from the stone,
The world and its mother go reeling
        and jigging forever
In answer to something that troubles
        the blood and the bone.

So I have to report there's no end
        to the song and the story,
With enough music in it to send us all
        drunk on our way;
As I go to my sleep I ask
        for a smile and a blessing:
'S a chara mo cléibh, bí meidhreach
        is gáirsiúil id' chré.

Farewell! But Whenever You Welcome the Hour
Thomas Moore

Farewell! but whenever you welcome the hour
That awakens the night-song of mirth in your
  bower,
Then think of the friend who once welcomed it
  too,
And forgot his own griefs to be happy with you.
His griefs may return — not a hope may remain
Of the few that have brighten'd his pathway of
  pain

But he ne'er will forget the short vision that threw
Its enchantment around him while ling'ring with
  you!

And still on that evening, when pleasure fills up
To the highest top sparkle each heart and each
  cup,
Where'er my path lies, be it gloomy or bright,
My soul, happy friends! shall be with you that
  night;
Shall join in your revels, your sports, and your
  wiles
And return to me beaming all o'er with your
  smiles! —

Too blest, if it tells me that, 'mid the gay cheer,
Some kind voice had murmur'd, 'I wish he were
  here!'
Let fate do her worst, there are relics of joy,
Bright dreams of the past, which she cannot
  destroy;
And which come, in the night-time, sorrow and
  care,
To bring back the features that joy used to wear.
Long, long be my heart with such memories fill'd!
Like the vase in which roses have once been distill'd —
You may break, you may ruin the vase, if you will,
But the scent of the roses will hang round it still.

Later On
Percy French

[Verse 1]

When we're children at our lessons, it is beautiful
  to think
Of the good time that is coming later on;
When we've done with silly copybooks and horrid
  pens and ink,
What a lovely time is coming later on!
The rivers of New Zealand, the mountains of
  Peru,
The watersheds of Europe, and the tribes of Tim-
  buctoo,
All the facts without the fancies, all the tiresome
  and true,
Will be nowhere in that lovely later on.

[Verse 5]

And so through all your lifetime you are longing
  for the day,
The lovely day that's coming later on;
When pens and ink and copybooks will all be laid
  away,
And that day is surely coming later on.
For when you're really tired, having done your
  level best,
When the story's nearly ended, and the sun sets in
  the West,

Then you'll lie down very gently, and the weary will
    find rest,
And I fancy we'll deserve it — later on.

Later on, later on,
Oh the many friends have gone,
Sweet lips that smiled and loving eyes that shone.
Through the darkness into light,
One by one they've winged their flight
And perhaps we'll play together — later on.

The Long Garden
Patrick Kavanagh

It was the garden of the golden apples,
A long garden between a railway and a road,
In the sow's rooting where the hen scratches
We dipped our fingers in the pockets of God.

In the thistly hedge old boots were flying sandals
By which we travelled through the childhood skies,
Old buckets rusty-holed with half-hung handles
Were drums to play when old men married wives.

The pole that lifted the clothes-line in the middle
Was the flag-pole on a prince's palace when
We looked at it through fingers crossed to riddle
In evening sunlight miracles for men.

It was the garden of the golden apples,
And when the Carrick train went by we knew
That we could never die till something happened
Like wishing for a fruit that never grew,

Or wanting to be up on Candle-Fort
Above the village with its shops and mill.
The racing cyclists' gasp-gapped reports
Hinted of pubs where life can drink his fill.

And when the sun went down into Drumcatton
And the New Moon by its little finger swung
From the telegraph wires, we knew how God had
    happened
And what the blackbird in the whitethorn sang.

It was the garden of the golden apples,
The half-way house where we had stopped a day
Before we took the west road to Drumcatton
Where the sun was always setting on the play.

The Last Rose of Summer
Thomas Moore

'Tis the last rose of summer left blooming alone;
all her lovely companions are faded and gone;
no flower of her kindred, no rose-bud is nigh,
to reflect back her blushes, or give sigh for sigh.

I'll not leave thee, thou lone one! to pine on the stem;
Since the lovely are sleeping, go, sleep thou with them.
Thus kindly I scatter thy leaves o'er the bed,
Where thy mates of the garden lie scentless and dead.

So soon may I follow, when friendships decay,
And from Love's shining circle the gems drop away.
When true hearts lie wither'd, and fond ones are flown,
Oh! who would inhabit this bleak world alone!

We never knew you old . . .

November Eve
[*To my mother*]
Michael Walsh

This is the twilight hour of long remembrance,
The heart's own memory night.
We never knew you old;
While yet the road
Wound through the Spring
And all the hills and skies
Gave back the laugh of life,
You went away leaving this green world lonely.

Since it is prayer alone
Can arch the Infinite,
'Tis thus we think of you
And so
Would we remembered be
By you the ever young!

Flower of Youth
Katharine Tynan

Lest Heaven be thronged with grey-beards hoary,
God, who made boys for His delight,
Stoops in a day of grief and glory
And calls them in, in from the night.
When they come trooping from the war
Our skies have many a new young star. ...

Dear boys! they shall be young forever.
The son of God was once a boy.
They run and leap by a clear river
And of their youth they have great joy.
God who made boys so clean and good
Smiles with the eyes of fatherhood.

Bereavement
Michael Walsh

Farewell! Farewell — beyond the farthest star
You went without goodbye!
And life is lonely as a desert place —
Its streams of joy run dry.

Ah! I shall seek in vain the countless crowds
That throng the market place —

Yea, walk o'er all the highways of the world,
But never see your face!

O love! those eyes are closed that watched with mine
The young unfolding year;
Its sweetest flower whose birth we hailed with hope
Now dies upon your bier.

When April comes to nurse the warm earth green
With sun and kindly rain,
White flowers will rise, but such a flower as you
Will never bloom again!

IN EXILE

I am of Ireland ...

The Irish Dancer
Anonymous [fourteenth century]

I am of Ireland,
And of the holy land
Of Ireland.
Good sir, pray I thee,
For of saint charity,
Come and dance with me
In Ireland.

She Is Far from the Land
Thomas Moore

She is far from the land where her young hero
   sleeps,
And lovers are round her sighing;
But coldly she turns from their gaze and weeps,
For her heart in his grave is lying!

She sings the wild song of her dear native plains,
Every note which he loved awaking;
Ah! little they think, who delight in her strains,
How the heart of the minstrel is breaking!

He had lived for his love, for his country he died;
They were all that to life had entwined him;
Nor soon shall the tears of his country be dried,
Nor long will his love stay behind him!

Oh! make her a grave where the sunbeams rest
When they promise a glorious morrow;
They'll shine o'er her sleep, like a smile from the
    west,
For her own loved island of sorrow.

In France
Francis Ledwidge

The silence of maternal hills
Is round me in my evening dreams;
And round me music-making bills
And mingling waves of pastoral streams.

Whatever way I turn I find
The path is old unto me still.
The hills of home are in my mind,
And there I wander as I will.

The Harbour
Winifred Letts

I think if I lay dying in some land
Where Ireland is no more than just a name,
My soul would travel back to find that strand
From whence it came.

I'd see the harbour in the evening light,
The old men staring at some distant ship,
The fishing-boats they fasten left and right
Beside the slip.

The sea-wrack lying on the wind-swept shore,
The grey thorn bushes growing in the sand,
Our Wexford coast from Arklow to Cahore —
My native land.

The little houses climbing up the hill,
Sea daisies growing in the sandy grass,
The tethered goats that wait large-eyed and still
To watch you pass.

The women at the well with dripping pails,
Their men colloguing by the harbour wall,
The coils of rope, the nets, the old brown sails
I know them all.

And then the Angelus — I'd surely see
The swaying bell against a golden sky,
So God, Who kept the love of home in me
Would let me die.

Galway Bay

If you ever go across the sea to Ireland,
Then maybe at the closing of your day
You will sit and watch the moon rise over Claddagh,
And watch the sun go down on Galway Bay.

Just to hear again the ripple of the trout stream,
The women in the meadows making hay,
And to sit beside a turf-fire in the cabin
And to watch the barefoot gossoons at their play.

For the breezes blowing o'er the seas from Ireland
Are perfumed by the heather as they blow
And the women in the uplands diggin' praties,
Speak a language that the strangers do not know.

For the strangers came and tried to teach us their
    way
They scorn'd us just for being what we are
But they might as well go chasing after moonbeams
Or light a penny candle from a star.

And if there's going to be a life hereafter,
And somehow I am sure there's going to be
I will ask my God to let me make my heaven
In that dear land across the Irish sea.

Bantry Bay

As I'm sitting all alone in the gloaming,
It might have been but yesterday
That we watched the fisher sails all homing
Till the little herring fleet at anchor lay.
Then the fisher girls with baskets swinging
Came running down the old stone way
Every lassie to her sailor lad was singing
A welcome back to Bantry Bay.

Then we heard the piper's sweet note tuning
And all the lassies turned to hear
As they mingled with a soft voice crooning
Till the music floated down the wooden pier.
'Save you kindly, colleens all,' said the piper
'Hands across and trip it while I play.'
And the tender sound of song and merry dancing
Stole softly over Bantry Bay.

As I'm sitting all alone in the gloaming
The shadows of the past draw near.
And I see the loving faces round me

That used to glad the old brown pier.
Some are gone upon their last lov'd homing,
Some are left, but they are old and grey.
And we're waiting for the tide in the gloaming
To sail upon the great highway
To the land of rest unending
All peacefully from Bantry Bay.

Gortnamona
Percy French

Long, long ago, in the woods of Gortnamona,
I thought the birds were singing in the blackthorn
    tree;
But oh! it was my heart that was ringing, ringing,
    ringing,
With the joy that you were bringing O my love, to me.

Long, long ago, in the woods of Gortnamona,
I thought the wind was sighing round the black-
    thorn tree;
But oh! it was the banshee that was crying, crying,
    crying,
And I knew my love was dying far across the sea.

Now if you go through the woods of Gortnamona,
You hear the raindrops creeping through the
    blackthorn tree,

But oh! it is the tears I am weeping, weeping,
  weeping,
For the loved one that is sleeping far away from
  me.

Dedication
Patrick MacGill

I speak with a proud tongue of the people who
  were
And the people who are,
The worthy of Ardara, the Rosses and Inishkeel,
My kindred —
The people of the hills and the dark-haired passes
My neighbours on the lift of the brae,
In the lap of the valley.

To them *Sláinte*!

I speak of the old men,
The wrinkle-rutted,
Who dodder about foot-weary —
For their day is as the day that has been and is no
  more —
Who warm their feet by the fire,
And recall memories of the times that are gone;
Who kneel in the lamplight and pray
For the peace that has been theirs —

And who beat one dry-veined hand against
    another
Even in the sun —
For the coldness of death is on them.

I speak of the old women
Who danced to yesterday's fiddle
And dance no longer.
They sit in a quiet place and dream
And see visions
Of what is to come,
Of their issue,
Which has blossomed to manhood and
    womanhood —
And seeing thus
They are happy
For the day that was leaves no regrets,
And peace is theirs,
And perfection.

I speak of the strong men
Who shoulder their burdens in the hot day,
Who stand on the market-place
And bargain in loud voices,
Showing their stock to the world.
Straight the glance of their eyes —
Broad-shouldered,
Supple.
Under their feet the holms blossom,

The harvest yields.
And their path is of prosperity.

I speak of the women,
Strong hipped, full-bosomed,
Who drive the cattle to graze at dawn,
Who milk the cows at dusk.
Grace in their homes,
And in the crowded ways
Modest and seemly —
Mother of children!

I speak of the children
Of the many townlands,
Blossoms of the Bogland,
Flowers of the Valley,
Who know not yesterday, nor to-morrow,
And are happy,
The pride of those who have begot them.

And thus it is,
Ever and always,
In Ardara, the Rosses and Inishkeel —
Here, as elsewhere,
The Weak, the Strong, and the Blossoming —
And thus my kindred.

To them *Sláinte*!

The Harp That Once through Tara's Halls
Thomas Moore

The harp that once through Tara's halls
The soul of music shed,
Now hangs as mute on Tara's walls
As if that soul were fled.
So sleeps the pride of former days,
So glory's thrill is o'er,
And hearts that once beat high for praise,
Now feel that pulse no more.

No more to chiefs and ladies bright
The harp of Tara swells:
The chord alone, that breaks at night,
Its tale of ruin tells.
Thus Freedom now so seldom wakes,
The only throb she gives,
Is when some heart indignant breaks,
To show that still she lives.

The Exile
Michael Walsh

There's many a far horizon line,
Blue waters ridged with foam,
Wild lonely wastes of sea and sky,
Between me and my home! —

The pastures fond and far away,
The daisies and the dew,
The morning land of light and mist —
Those summers that I knew.

The long green hours of grass and sun,
The blue and peaceful air
Are lost beyond the sky and sea,
As if they never were!

Shall death's horizon line unveil
The fields of memory —
The misty hills that close around
The land that cradled me?

Connemara Cradle Song

On wings of the wind o'er the dark rolling deep
Angels are coming to watch o'er thy sleep,
Angels are coming to watch over thee,
So list to the wind coming over the sea.

[Chorus:]
Hear the wind blow, love,
Hear the wind blow.
Lean your head over
And hear the wind blow.

Oh winds of the night, may your fury be crossed,
May no one that's dear to our island be lost.
Blow the wind gently, calm be the foam,
Shine the light brightly to guide them home.
[Chorus]

The currachs are sailing way out on the blue,
Laden with herring of silvery hue.
Silver the herring and silver the sea,
And soon there'll be silver for baby and me.
[Chorus]

The currachs tomorrow will stand on the shore
And Daddy goes sailing, sailing no more.
The nets will be drying, the nets heaven blessed,
And safe in my arms, dear, contented he'll rest.
[Chorus]

The Meeting of the Waters
Thomas Moore

There is not in the wide world a valley so sweet
As that vale in whose bosom the bright waters meet;
Oh! the last rays of feeling and life must depart,
Ere the bloom of that valley shall fade from my heart.

Yet it was not that nature had shed o'er the scene
Her purest of crystal and brightest of green;

'Twas not her soft magic of streamlet or hill,
Oh! no — it was something more exquisite still.

'Twas that friends, the belov'd of my bosom, were
    near,
Who made every dear scene of enchantment more
    dear,
And who felt how the best charms of nature
    improve,
When we see them reflected from looks that we love.

Sweet vale of Avoca! How calm could I rest
In thy bosom of shade, with the friends I love best,
Where the storms that we feel in this cold world
    should cease,
And our hearts, like thy waters, be mingled in peace.

Stanzas to Erin
J J Callanan

Still green are thy mountains and bright is thy shore,
And the voice of thy fountains is heard as of yore:
The sun o'er thy valleys, dear Erin, shines on,
Though thy bard and thy lover forever is gone.

Nor shall he, an exile, thy glad scenes forget —
The friends fondly loved, ne'er again to be met —

The glens where he mused on the deeds of his
   nation,
And waked his young harp with wild inspiration.

Still, still, though between us may roll the broad
   ocean,
Will I cherish thy name with the same deep devotion;
And though minstrels more brilliant my place may
   supply,
None loves you more fondly, more truly than I.

The Green Glens of Antrim

[Verses 1 and 2]
Far across yonder blue lies a true fairy land,
Where the sea ripples over the shingles and sand,
Where the gay honeysuckle is luring the bee,
And the green glens of Antrim are calling to me.

And if only you knew how the light of the moon
Turns a blue Irish lake to a silver lagoon,
You'd imagine a picture of heav'n it would be,
Where the green glens of Antrim are calling to me.

*May the road rise
to meet you ...*

May the Road Rise to Meet You ...

May the road rise to meet you
May the wind be always at your back
May the sun shine warm upon your face,
The rains fall soft upon your fields
And until we meet again
May God hold you in the hollow of His hand.

[In the original Irish:]
Go n-éirí an bóthar leat
Go raibh an ghaoth go brách ag do chúl
Go lonraí an ghrian go te ar d'aghaidh
Go dtite an bháisteach go mín ar do pháirceanna
Agus go mbuailimid le chéile arís,
Go gcoinní Dia i mbos A láimhe thú.

Traditional Blessing

May the blessing of the Earth be on you —
the great round earth; may you ever have a
kindly greeting for them you pass as you're
going along the roads.

May the earth be soft under you when you
rest upon it, tired at the end of the day, and may
it rest easy over you when, at the last, you lay
out under it;

May it rest so lightly over you, that your soul
may be out from under it quickly, and up, and
off, and on its way to God.

In Time of Sorrow ...

May you see God's light on the path ahead
When the road you walk is dark.
May you always hear,
Even in your hour of sorrow,
The gentle singing of the lark.
When times are hard may hardness
Never turn your heart to stone,
May you always remember
when the shadows fall —
You do not walk alone.

Be Thou my vision . . .

Rop Tú Mo Bhaile / Be Thou My Vision
[Early Irish] Translated by Mary Byrne
Versified by Eleanor Hull (altd.)

Be thou my vision, O Lord of my heart,
naught be all else to me, save that thou art;
thou my best thought in the day and the night,
waking or sleeping, thy presence my light.

Be thou my wisdom, be thou my true word,
I ever with thee, and thou with me, Lord;
thou my great Father, and I thy true heir;
thou in me dwelling, and I in thy care.

Be thou my breast-plate, my sword for the fight;
be thou my armour, and be thou my might;
thou my soul's shelter, and thou my high tower,
raise thou me heavenward, O Power of my power.

Riches I heed not, nor vain empty praise,
thou mine inheritance through all my days;
thou, and thou only, the first in my heart,
High King of heaven, my treasure thou art!

High King of heaven, when the battle is done,
grant heaven's joy to me, O bright heaven's sun,
Christ of my own heart, whatever befall,
still be my vision, O Ruler of all.

Lead, Kindly Light
John Henry Newman

Lead, kindly Light, amid th'encircling gloom,
Lead Thou me on!
The night is dark, and I am far from home;
Lead Thou me on!
Keep Thou my feet; I do not ask to see
The distant scene: one step enough for me.

I was not ever thus, nor prayed that Thou
Shouldst lead me on;
I loved to choose and see my path; but now
Lead Thou me on!
I loved the garish day, and, spite of fears,
Pride ruled my will: remember not past years!

So long Thy power hath blessed me, sure it still,
Will lead me on.
O'er moor and fen, o'er crag and torrent, till
The night is gone;
And with the morn those angel faces smile,
Which I have loved long since, and lost awhile!

Meantime, along the narrow rugged path,
Thyself hast trod,
Lead, Saviour, lead me home in childlike faith,
Home to my God.
To rest forever after earthly strife
In the calm light of everlasting life.

Alone With None But Thee, My God
Attributed to St Columba; Translation Anonymous

Alone with none but thee, my God,
I journey on my way;
What need I fear, when thou art near,
O King of night and day?
More safe am I within thy hand,
Than if a host did round me stand.

My destined time is fixed by thee,
And Death doth know his hour.
Did warriors strong around me throng,
They could not stay his power;

No walls of stone can man defend
When thou thy messenger dost send.

My life I yield to thy decree,
And bow to thy control
In peaceful calm, for from thine arm
No power can wrest my soul.
Could earthly omens e'er appal
A man that heeds the heavenly call!

The child of God can fear no ill,
His chosen dread no foe;
We leave our fate with thee, and wait
Thy bidding when to go.
'Tis not from chance our comfort springs,
Thou art our trust, O King of kings.

It Were My Soul's Desire
[Old Irish] Versified Eleanor Hull

It were my soul's desire
To see the face of God;
It were my soul's desire
To rest in his abode.

It were my soul's desire
A spirit free from gloom,
It were my soul's desire
New life beyond the doom.

It were my soul's desire
To study zealously;
This, too, my soul's desire,
A clear rule set for me.

Grant, Lord, my soul's desire,
Deep waves of cleansing sighs,
Grant, Lord, my soul's desire,
From earthly cares to rise.

It were my soul's desire
To shun the doom of hell;
Yet more my soul's desire
Within his house to dwell.

It were my soul's desire
To imitate my king,
It were my soul's desire
His endless praise to sing.

It were my soul's desire
When heaven's gate is won,
To find my soul's desire,
Clear shining like the sun.

This still my soul's desire
Whatever life afford,
To gain my soul's desire
And see thy face, O Lord.

Ag Críost an Síol
[Old Irish]

Ag Críost an síol, ag Críost an fomhar;
in iothlainn Dé go dtugtar sinn.

Ag Críost an mhuir, ag Críost an t-iasc;
i líonta Dé go gcastar sinn.

Ó fhás go haois, ó aois go bás,
do dhá láimh a Chríost, anall tharainn.

Ó bhás go críoch nach críoch ach athfhás,
i bParthas na ngrás go rabhaimid.

Translation: Thomas Kinsella

To Christ the seed, to Christ the crop,
in barn of Christ may we be brought.

To Christ the sea, to Christ the fish,
in nets of Christ may we be caught.

From growth to age, from age to death,
Thy two arms here, O Christ, about us.

From death to end — not end but growth —
in blessed Paradise may we be.

Two Prayers
Traditional
Translated by Eleanor Hull

I rest with Thee, O Jesus,
And do Thou rest with me.
The oil of Christ on my poor soul,
The creed of the Twelve to make me whole,
Above my head I see.
O Father, who created me,
O Son, who purchased me,
O Spirit Blest, who blessest me,
Rest ye with me.

     *   *   *

I lie down with God, and may God lie down with
   me;
The right hand of God under my head,
The two hands of Mary round about me,
The cross of the nine white angels
From the back of my head
To the sole of my feet.
May I not lie with evil,
And may evil not lie with me.

All Things Bright and Beautiful
Cecil Alexander

All things bright and beautiful,
All creatures great and small,
All things wise and wonderful;
The Lord God made them all.

Each little flower that opens,
Each little bird that sings,
He made their glowing colours,
He made their tiny wings.

The rich man in his castle,
The poor man at his gate,
He made them, high or lowly,
And ordered their estate.

The purple-headed mountain,
The river running by,
The sunset and the morning,
That brightens up the sky;

The cold wind in the winter,
The pleasant summer sun,
The ripe fruits in the garden –
He made them every one.

The tall trees in the greenwood,
The meadows for our play,
The rushes by the water
To gather every day;

He gave us eyes to see them,
And lips that we might tell,
How great is God Almighty,
Who has made all things well.

Between God and His right hand ...

An Phaidir Gheal
Traditional

Cá luífidh tú anocht?
Idir Muire is a Mac,
idir Bríd is a brat,
idir Colmcille is a sciath,
idir Dia is a lámh dheas.

Translation: Thomas Kinsella

Where will you lie tonight?
Between Mary and her Son
between Bridget and her cloak
between Colm Cille and his shield
between God and His right hand.

Morning Prayer from Connemara
Traditional
Translated by Douglas Hyde

The will of God be done by us.
The law of God be kept by us,
Our evil will controlled by us,
Our tongue in check be held by us,
Repentance timely made by us,
Christ's passion understood by us,
Each sinful crime be shunned by us,
Much on the *End* be mused by us,
And Death be blessed found by us,
With Angels' music heard by us,
And God's high praise sung by us,
For ever and aye.

Litany (Liodán an Rísigh)
Seán Ó Cearbhaill

[Response:
Déan trócaire is trua]

In the tears of the broken
When no word is spoken
O God of all tokens
Déan trócaire is trua.

In the night of my sorrow
Some hope I will borrow
From the God of tomorrow
Déan trócaire is trua.

In the time of leaving
When an end comes to grieving
Dear Lord of Believing
Déan trócaire is trua.

Saint Patrick's Breastplate [extract]
Traditional

Christ beside me,
Christ before me,
Christ behind me,

Christ within me,
Christ beneath me,
Christ above me,

Christ on my right hand,
Christ on my left,

Christ where I lie,
Christ where I sit,
Christ where I rise.

Christ in the hearts of all who think of me,
Christ in the mouths of all who speak to me,
Christ in every eye that sees me,
Christ in every ear that hears me.

Today I put on
a terrible strength,
invoking the Trinity,
confessing the Three,
with faith in the One
as I face my Maker.

I See His Blood Upon the Rose
Joseph Mary Plunkett

I see his blood upon the rose
And in the stars the glory of his eyes,
His body gleams amid eternal snows,
His tears fall from the skies.

I see his face in every flower;
The thunder and the singing of the birds
Are but his voice — and carven by his power
Rocks are his written words.

All pathways by his feet are worn,
His strong heart stirs the ever-beating sea,
His crown of thorns is twined with every thorn,
His cross is every tree.

At Sunset
Michael Walsh

I often watch the setting sun,
Its sinking nimbus growing less
And colour into colour run
In unimagined loveliness.

What lands within those western fires!
What gleaming seas and cities old!
What gilded pinnacles and spires!
What labyrinths and courts of gold!

    *   *   *

Dear God, when weary with the days
And evening skies are over me,
By ships of cloud and sunset bays
Shall I at last go home to Thee?

Pied Beauty
Gerard Manley Hopkins

Glory be to God for dappled things —
For skies of couple-colour as a brindled cow;
For rose-moles all in stipple upon trout that
    swim;
Fresh-firecoal chestnut-falls; finches' wings;

Landscape plotted and pieced — fold, fallow, and
  plough;
And all trades, their gear and tackle and trim.

All things counter, original, spare, strange;
Whatever is fickle, freckled (who knows how?)
With swift, slow; sweet, sour; adazzle, dim;
He fathers-forth whose beauty is past change:
Praise him.

O Lord, Support Us All the Day Long
John Henry Newman

O Lord, support us all the day long,
until the shadows lengthen,
and the evening comes,
and the busy world is hushed,
and the fever of life is over,
and our work is done.

Then in your mercy,
grant us a safe lodging and a holy rest,
and peace at the last.
Amen

PART II

Reflection

Peace comes dropping slow ...

The Lake Isle of Innisfree
W B Yeats

I will arise and go now, and go to Innisfree,
And a small cabin build there, of clay and wattles
  made:
Nine bean-rows will I have there, a hive for the
  honey-bee,
And live alone in the bee-loud glade.

And I shall have some peace there, for peace
  comes dropping slow,
Dropping from the veils of the morning to where
  the cricket sings;
There midnight's all a glimmer, and noon a
  purple glow,
And evening full of the linnet's wings.

I will arise and go now, for always night and day
I hear lake water lapping with low sounds by the
  shore;

While I stand on the roadway, or on the pavements
    grey,
I hear it in the deep heart's core.

The Left Shoe
Mary Rose Callan

In the parlour after the funeral
nuns offer sandwiches, finely-cut,
say they've lost their sister-in-Christ.

Mother listens for a footstep
passing the door,
holds tears for her sister back.

They give us a suitcase.
Personal things. Light as her arm
in the crook of mine

the last time she shopped for shoes —
calfskin, soft and crinkled,
the size as small as a child's.

We find it without its companion
jumbled
with medals and clothes —

her life
swept into a suitcase —
the price attached to the sole.

In the Shadows
Francis Ledwidge

The silent music of the flowers
Wind-mingled shall not fail to cheer
The lonely hours
When I no more am here.

Then in some shady willow place
Take up the book my heart has made,
And hide your face
Against my name which was a shade.

Hereafter
[i.m. my mother]
Áine Miller

I wish you
Then wish you wouldn't
Follow me around. Everywhere
You're there, every time I turn,
Breathing down my neck.
Beyond the beyond, I say. Wasn't it you

Who taught me to sidestep,
Let my angel guardian go before
Into that top room,
Draw their fire? Light swording
From the landing,
I'd make a run for it

Across that shuttered room.
Shadows folded
Alongside
In the space between me,
Eiderdown and wall,
I feathered into dream. Tomorrow

When I wish you
And before I wish you wouldn't
Follow me upstairs,
Flapping at my heels,
I'll step aside
On this last flight,

Let you pass on.
You may go gently.
The room beyond
Holds no terrors for you
After all this time. I shall follow
In, then nestle into peace.

The Sunlight on the Garden
Louis MacNeice

The sunlight on the garden
Hardens and grows cold,
We cannot cage the minute
Within its nets of gold,
When all is told
We cannot beg for pardon.

Our freedom as free lances
Advances towards its end;
The earth compels, upon it
Sonnets and birds descend;
And soon, my friend,
We shall have no time for dances.

The sky was good for flying
Defying the church bells
And every evil iron
Siren and what it tells:
The earth compels,
We are dying, Egypt, dying

And not expecting pardon,
Hardened in heart anew,
But glad to have sat under
Thunder and rain with you,
And grateful too
For sunlight on the garden.

Heaven-Haven
Gerard Manley Hopkins

I have desired to go
Where springs not fail,
To fields where flies no sharp and sided hail
And a few lilies blow.

And I have asked to be
Where no storms come,
Where the green swell is in the havens dumb,
And out of the swing of the sea.

Jill's Death
George Buchanan

After Jill died they remembered how she liked this
    chair,
her jokes about an ornament in the corner.
They did not trek mournfully to the cemetery
with its array of crosses at the border of the town.
They called some flowerbeds in the garden Jill's beds,
and said 'How are Jill's flowers today?' and went
outside and looked at them. The flowers swayed
or hardly moved in the slight wind. This
perfection spoke of the exact nature of life,
with undismayed joyfulness.

Lightning
Paul Murray

In the fissure of the moment,
in the sudden lightning
of God's mercy

the saint
is indistinguishable
from the sinner,

and the flowers of earth
and the flowers of heaven
are the same.

When
George Russell (AE)

When mine hour is come
Let no teardrop fall
And no darkness hover
Round me where I lie
Let the vastness call
One who was its lover,
Let me breathe the sky.

Where the lordly light
Walks along the world,
And its silent tread
Leaves the grasses bright,
Leaves the flowers uncurled,
Let me to the dead
Breathe a gay goodnight.

Elegy at Mornington
Padraig J Daly

There are a few houses near the church,
Smoke comes from chimneys;

Here is quiet countryside,
Flat and undisturbed
Since the first voyagers.

Beyond the church
Old gravestones stand out against the sky.

Out there the estuary,
A causeway to the tide,
Vast mudspaces, seabirds;

A curlew is calling your name.

This morning the church was cold;
I knelt silently to remember you.

From nowhere
Gold light began to flood through windows,

Sparking the brass candlesticks,
Cutting the altarcloth in two,

Lighting the virgin in her niche,
Following the bright grains of the wood.

In its liberality,
I make it your parable.

There is always something happening
Along the estuary:

Seeping of water,
Yellow flowers opening,
Birds descending in noisy flocks,

Appearing, disappearing,
Making figures of eight in the sky;

And youngsters always
Searching for something beautiful and strange.

You called your daughter Catherine,
Your happiness at her birth
A blazing, circling wheel of praise.

Nowadays she begins to walk;
She has taken over your smile,
Your sudden laughter;

And in this Summer light
I watch her clap her hands at songbirds
With your same wonder.

In the flat lands beyond your house
Swans call across the air,

The sands have covered over
The ruins of limestone castles.

Your house is sheltered by tall trees,
Your kitchen door opens onto meadows;
Horses in the distance race through yellow fields.

And nowadays your husband, for your sake,
Tends the desert of your garden
Into abundant fruitfulness.

Ashes
Jean O'Brien

They did not look like ashes,
Not the dry grey papery type anyway.
They were more like something gardeners
know, grey and white bonemeal, but
then gardeners know too the brown
earth and how it remakes itself
from old roots, faded flowers,
fallen leaves, twigs and even bones —
it is all fodder to the earth.

I will remember this when the skies lighten
and the sun moves up.
When spring comes I will search
the ground for the first pushing
tip of the tulip bulbs planted
last November. Hidden under a drift
of leaves the shoots of what
will be daffodils, and on the dry
branches of the rose bush, tiny
green nodes will break the surface.

Sometime in the evening after
the work is done, I will walk out
into the garden and watch it
display itself. I'll think
of the heavy brown urn we buried

in the earth, and know he was
only turning back on himself,
for after his lifetime where else
could he go?

Creed
Conleth Ellis

Though a moon that shone
Ivory in a north sky
Roughly washed with lye
Has all but gone,

A cloud's edge says, Faith
Is the only prayer
To countenance despair;
Know by the fading wraith

In the branches' snare
That the sun turns
Still and the dark burns
Into the light somewhere.

Four Ducks on a Pond
William Allingham

Four ducks on a pond,
A grass bank beyond,
A blue sky of spring,
White birds on the wing:
What a little thing
To remember for years —
To remember with tears!

Wild Apple Time
Michael Walsh

In the hawthorn fields
It is wild apple time.
Red lips and pale brow,
Where, where are you now,
In the wild apple time?

In the hawthorn fields
How the trees shed their gold
On the green aftergrass;
How the years — my years — pass
And my life sheds its gold.

*   *   *

In the hawthorn fields
It is wild apple time.
Wide seas and long years
Have left me but tears
For the wild apple time!

Shell
Brendan Kennelly

I cannot say I came from nothing
But so it seemed when the sea
Began to shape me. How long

It took is not important.
Light and dark passed through me.
Nothing was constant

But the labouring
Fingers of the sea
At their grind of love and making.

This happened where few
Would wish to penetrate
And none could see

But I received my body there
And hid within me
All the voices of my maker

Singing of his work
As I lurched and tumbled
Through the unfathomed dark.

I bear, I am forever borne.
I am complete yet I must turn
And spin with the deep will, a form

Content to be
The still, perfect image of the sea
Or its demented plaything in a storm.

The Wayfarer
Pádraic Pearse

The beauty of the world hath made me sad,
This beauty that will pass;
Sometimes my heart hath shaken with great joy
To see a leaping squirrel in a tree,
Or a red lady-bird upon a stalk,
Or little rabbits in a field at evening,
Lit by a slanting sun,
Or some green hill where shadows drifted by,
Some quiet hill where mountainy men hath sown
And soon would reap, near to the gate of Heaven;
Or children with bare feet upon the sands
Of some ebbed sea, or playing on the streets
Of little towns in Connacht,

Things young and happy.
And then my heart hath told me:
These will pass,
Will pass and change, will die and be no more,
Things bright and green, things young and happy;
And I have gone upon my way
Sorrowful.

In Memory of Patrick Boyle, 1905-1982
Francis Harvey

It was snowing in Glenveagh the day you
died, Moylenanav was white, and the red
deer watched us through fluted curtains of flowered
light; the torrents were writhing like serpents
in the heather and the waterfalls hung
out of the sky like the entrails of clouds;
the wind was skinning the boles of birches
and peeling the scabs of lichen from
the scalps of the stones and we were cold
that day as we ate our brown bread and cheese
under a dripping rhododendron but
not as cold as you were, Patrick Boyle, had
we known it then, laid out on your bed
on the far side of Ireland.
            The deer turned their
beautiful buff-coloured rumps into
the wind and one stag with antlers twisting

out of its head like a thornbush out of
a split crag paused for a moment to stare
at us out of eyes as impenetrable
and mysterious as the wilderness
in which it was bred.
                    I remembered those
eyes when they told me, Patrick Boyle, that you
were dead and how you looked at me that last
time I saw you alive with the eyes of
a stag being hunted towards the ultimate
wilderness for which we are all bred.

Unapprehended
Eithne Strong

Dark song arose.
Black
out of the black clefts,
borne out of the rock's upheaved jag.
Primaeval
before any knowing —
holding between the balancing stars
out beyond the rim of all things
beat dark song.
Old song, before ever was life
was the beat of song:
old beat of the life-thought;
strong heavy beat to shatter through

my flesh now
and shake to drenching sobs
what holds the shape of me.
Beat on beat
where is life is beat
of old sadness going back
and back
and then on and on.

A Soft Day
Winifred Letts

A soft day, thank God!
A wind from the south
With a honeyed mouth;
A scent of drenching leaves,
Briar and beech and lime,
White elder-flower and thyme
And the soaking grass smells sweet,
Crushed by my two bare feet,
While the rain drips,
Drips, drips, drips from the eaves.

A soft day, thank God!
The hills wear a shroud
Of silver cloud;
The web the spider weaves
Is a glittering net;

The woodland path is wet,
And the soaking earth smells sweet
Under my two bare feet,
And the rain drips,
Drips, drips, drips from the leaves.

Crewbawn
Francis Ledwidge

White clouds that change and pass,
And stars that shine awhile,
Dew water on the grass,
A fox upon a stile.

A river broad and deep,
A slow boat on the waves,
My sad thoughts on the sleep
That hollows out the graves.

After You Are Gone
Michael Walsh

I think that I shall never want to see
Those fields when you are gone — those hard high hills
With which you wrestled early, late, and long,
That I might share with you their scanty yield,

That I might grow and live and give mankind
A few brief songs! — I shall not want to see
Grey stubble in the field of last year's corn —
That crop that you had sown before you died!

Nor that long path that dips and rises through
Those quiet acres sloping from the door,
That path you made with swift and lightsome feet
Through this and other fields unto her home,
In that bright year, in that enchanted year
When youth was rich and singing in its soul.
(Ah! singing till she went for all her grace —
Went in the primrose time of life and love!)

Where You Are
Sheila O'Hagan

I know the country you are in
is near. Around me linger whispers,
a supernal scent, and the way
you once put your hand on my head
happens again and again.

I know your eyes will still be sad,
your hands inclined to wring themselves
into solutions. I couldn't hold you back
nor follow you into dark.

But I say to you this night,
whatever you feel or hear or see
tell me; whatever country you are in,
be there for me, all mother bright,
and welcoming.

Immortality
Susan Mitchell

Age cannot reach me where the veils of God
    Have shut me in,
For me the myriad births of stars and suns
    Do but begin,
And here how fragrantly there blows to me
    The holy breath,
Sweet from the flowers and stars and the hearts of men,
    From life and death. ...

Awhile we walk the world on its wide roads
    and narrow ways,
And they pass by, the countless shadowy groups
    of nights and days;
We know them not, O happy heart,
    For you and I
Watch where within a slow dawn lightens up
    Another sky.

The Parting
Sara Berkeley

I
You lower my emotions, sealed in their casket,
To the sea bed, knowing I have nothing to say
Paring down to presence and absence
The sad abstractions of our last day
My throat grows heavy between your hands
My heart gets tossed away.

2
A shadow is working hard against the night
Working furiously on a morning wall
The shadow cast by fifteen beams of light
I am a child's bright stone
Longing to be the weapon of your fight
I am the fifteen beams coming straight down.

3
In brief moments when a nerve winks out
It seems as though you will always be there
The heart kicks — and then you are removed
You are climbing down the angry white stairs
You are the shadow resting on my skin
And we, a double splash of oars into the still air.

The Distant Pier
Paul Murray

How it is that words then said
and silences we kept
on that occasion have given
shape and meaning to my solitude
I cannot explain.

It was late in the afternoon,
I remember,
and we were walking at our ease
back and forth
on the grey, granite pier
near Ostia Antica,
with then, as now, only
the sound of your words
— not the shape, not the meaning —
distinct in my ear.

But those words, your words,
remain like music in my solitude,
and the sound of your voice
is like clear water lapping
and breaking
against the prow of my mind.

Age of Exploration
Conleth Ellis

Now suddenly on your map
I have no coordinates.
Somewhere to the left
Under the western angel's
Blast from puffed cheeks
Where the cartographer wrote
HERE BE MONSTERS
I have been banished.

Another dark age begins
And there is no anticipating
The ritual preparations
For a voyage of discovery.
There must be endless ruined delay
Before our hearts' conquistadores
Find for themselves a country
Beyond the intimacies of love.

Nor will this mark the end
Of our probing of bounds.
Is there a coast of a sixth
Continent to be charted and
Are there fathoms still to be set
Against an eight sea's shoals?
Best if love map out its course
Only as far as the edges of hope.

To Mona
Michael Walsh

I met you on an April day;
That day will never die!
Its winds and clouds are with me yet;
Its setting sun that will not set,
Below a memoried sky.

And clearer grows that April day
As other days go past—
All other days go one by one
Into the night's oblivion
But this fond day will last!

And Then No More
James Clarence Mangan

[Verses 1 and 2]

I saw her once, one little while, and then no more:
'Twas Eden's light on Earth awhile, and then no more.
Amid the throng she passed along the meadow-floor:
Spring seemed to smile on Earth awhile, and then
   no more:
But whence she came, which way she went, what
   garb she wore
I noted not; I gazed awhile, and then no more!

I saw her once, one little while, and then no more:
'Twas Paradise on Earth awhile, and then no more.
Ah! What avail my vigils pale, my magic lore?
She shone before mine eyes awhile, and then no more.
The shallop of my peace is wrecked on Beauty's shore.
Near Hope's fair isle it rode awhile, and then no
    more!

Autobiography
Louis MacNeice

In my childhood trees were green
And there was plenty to be seen.

Come back early or never come.

My father made the walls resound,
He wore his collar the wrong way round.

Come back early or never come.

My mother wore a yellow dress;
Gentle, gently, gentleness.

Come back early or never come.

When I was five the black dreams came;
Nothing after was quite the same.

Come back early or never come.

The dark was talking to the dead;
The lamp was dark beside my bed.

Come back early or never come.

When I woke they did not care;
Nobody, nobody was there.

Come back early or never come.

When my silent terror cried,
Nobody, nobody replied.

Come back early or never come.

I got up; the chilly sun
Saw me walk away alone.

Come back early or never come.

Be Still As You Are Beautiful
Patrick MacDonogh

Be still as you are beautiful
Be silent as the rose;
Through miles of starlit countryside
Unspoken worship flows
To reach you in your loveless room
From lonely men whom daylight gave
The blessing of your passing face
Impenetrably grave.

A white owl in the lichened wood
Is circling silently,
More secret and more silent yet
Must be your love to me.
Thus, while about my dreaming head
Your soul in ceaseless vigil goes,
Be still as you are beautiful
Be silent as the rose.

We Parted In Silence
Isabella Valancy Crawford

We parted in silence, we parted by night,
On the banks of that lonely river;
Where the fragrant limes their boughs unite,
We met — and we parted forever!
The night-bird sung, and the stars above
Told many a touching story,
Of friends long passed to the kingdom of love,
Where the soul wears its mantle of glory.

We parted in silence,— our cheeks were wet
With the tears that were past controlling;
We vowed we would never, no, never forget,
And those vows at the time were consoling;
But those lips that echoed the sounds of mine
Are as cold as that lonely river;
And that eye, that beautiful spirit's shrine,
Has shrouded its fires forever.

And now on the midnight sky I look,
And my heart grows full of weeping;
Each star is to me a sealèd book,
Some tale of that loved one keeping.
We parted in silence — we parted in tears,
On the banks of that lonely river:
But the odour and bloom of those bygone years
Shall hang o'er its waters forever.

Requiescat
Oscar Wilde

Tread lightly, she is near
Under the snow,
Speak gently, she can hear
The daisies grow.

All her bright golden hair
Tarnished with rust,
She that was young and fair
Fallen to dust.

Lily-like, white as snow,
She hardly knew
She was a woman, so
Sweetly she grew.

Coffin-board, heavy stone,
Lie on her breast,
I vex my heart alone,
She is at rest.

Peace, Peace, she cannot hear
Lyre or sonnet,
All my life's buried here,
Heap earth upon it.

Fornocht do Chonac Thú / Ideal
Pádraic Pearse
Translated by Thomas McDonagh

Fornocht do chonac thú,
a áille na háille,
is do dhallas mo shúil
ar eagla go stánfainn.

Do chualas do cheol,
a bhinne na binne,
is do dhúnas mo chluas
ar eagla go gclisfinn.

Do bhlaiseas do bhéal,
a mhilse na milse,
is do chruas mo chroí
ar eagla mo mhillte.

Do dhallas mo shúil,
is mo chluas do dhúnas;
do chruas mo chroí,
is mo mhian do mhúchas.

Do thugas mo chúl
ar an aisling do chumas,
's ar an ród so romham
m'aghaidh do thugas.

Do thugas mo ghnúis
ar an ród so romham,
ar an ngníomh do chim,
's ar an mbás do gheobhad.

Naked I saw thee,
O beauty of beauty!
And I blinded my eyes
For fear I should flinch.

I heard thy music,
O sweetness of sweetness!
And I shut my ears
For fear I should fail.

I kissed thy lips
O sweetness of sweetness!
And I hardened my heart
For fear of my ruin.

I blinded my eyes
And my ears I shut,
I hardened my heart,
And my love I quenched.

I turned my back
On the dream I had shaped,
And to this road before me
My face I turned.

I set my face
To the road here before me,
To the work that I see,
To the death that I shall meet.

After My Last Song
Francis Ledwidge

Where I shall rest when my last song is over
The air is smelling like a feast of wine;
And purple breakers of the windy clover
Shall roll to cool this burning brow of mine;
And there shall come to me, when day is told
The peace of sleep when I am grey and old.

I'm wild for wandering to the far-off places
Since one forsook me whom I held most dear.
I want to see new wonders and new faces
Beyond East seas; but I will win back here
When my last song is sung, and veins are cold
As thawing snow, and I am grey and old.

Oh paining eyes, but not with salty weeping,
My heart is like a sod in winter rain;
Ere you will see those baying waters leaping
Like hungry hounds once more, how many a pain
Shall heal; but when my last short song is trolled
You'll sleep here on wan cheeks grown thin and old.

Deirdre's Lament for the Sons of Usnach
[From the Irish]
Translated by Samuel Ferguson

The lions of the hill are gone,
And I am left alone — alone —
Dig the grave both wide and deep,
For I am sick, and fain would sleep!

The falcons of the wood are flown,
And I am left alone — alone —
Dig the grave both deep and wide,
And let us slumber side by side. ...

Lament for Thomas McDonagh
Francis Ledwidge

He shall not hear the bittern cry
In the wild sky, where he is lain,
Nor voices of the sweeter birds
Above the wailing of the rain.

Nor shall he know when loud March blows
Thro' slanting snows her fanfare shrill,
Blowing to flame the golden cup
Of many an upset daffodil.

But when the Dark Cow leaves the moor
And pastures poor with greedy weeds,
Perhaps he'll hear her low at morn
Lifting her horn in pleasant meads.

The Waves of Breffny
Eva Gore-Booth

The grand road from the mountain goes shining
  to the sea,
And there is traffic on it and many a horse and cart,
But the little roads of Cloonagh are dearer far to me
And the little roads of Cloonagh go rambling
  through my heart.

A great storm from the ocean goes shouting o'er
  the hill,
And there is glory in it; and terror on the wind:
But the haunted air of twilight is very strange and still,
And the little winds of twilight are dearer to my mind.

The great waves of the Atlantic sweep storming on
  their way,
Shining green and silver with the hidden herring
  shoal;
But the little waves of Breffny have drenched my
  heart in spray,
And the little waves of Breffny go stumbling
  through my soul.

At Evening
Francis Ledwidge

A broad field at a wood's high end,
Daylight out and the stars half lit,
And let the dark-winged bat go flit
About the river's wide blue bend.
But thoughts of someone once a friend
Shall be calling loud thro' the hills of time.

Wide is the back-door of the Past
And I shall be leaving the slated town.
But no, the rain will be slanting brown
And large drops chasing the small ones fast
Down the wide pane, for a cloud was cast
On youth when he started the world to climb.

There won't be song, for song has died.
There won't be flowers for the flowers are done.
I shall see the red of a large cold sun
Wash down on the slow blue tide,
Where the noiseless deep fish glide
In the dark wet shade of the heavy lime.

One Final Gift
D H Cramer

Scatter me not to the restless winds
Nor toss my ashes to the sea.
Remember now those years gone by
When loving gifts I gave to thee.
Remember now the happy times
The family ties are shared.
Don't leave my resting place unmarked
As though you never cared.
Deny me not one final gift
For all who came to see.
A simple lasting proof that says
I loved and you loved me.

Lines written on a Seat on the Grand Canal, Dublin
'Erected to the Memory of Mrs Dermot O'Brien'
Patrick Kavanagh

O commemorate me where there is water,
Canal water preferably, so stilly
Greeny at the heart of summer. Brother
Commemorate me thus beautifully.
Where by a lock niagarously roars
The falls for those who sit in the tremendous
    silence

Of mid-July. No one will speak in prose
Who finds his way to these Parnassian islands.
A swan goes by head low with many apologies,
Fantastic light looks through the eyes of bridges —
And look! a barge comes bringing from Athy
And other far-flung towns mythologies.
O commemorate me with no hero-courageous
Tomb — just a canal-bank seat for the passer-by.

Homage to the Void
Paul Murray

[Verse 1]
The first glimpse
of you — I remember —
was of something perilous
yet lovely.
You were like a source
that had no beginning,
like a spring welling up
in the eyes of oblivion.
And so perilous you seemed
and so intolerably lovely
I thought to myself:
'It is a dream
it is no more than that'.

On Living Life to the Full
Paul Murray

When your heart is empty
and your hands are empty

you can take into your hands
the gift of the present

you can experience in your heart
the moment in its fullness.

*   *   *

And this you will know,
though perhaps you may not yet
understand it,

this you will know:

that nothing
of all you have longed for
or have sought to hold fast
can relieve you of your thirst,
your loneliness,

until you learn
to take in your hands
and raise to your lips

this cup of solitude
this chalice of the void

and drain it to the dregs.

Night Air
Sheila O'Hagan

I love your walking in on me each night,
Not the usual wisp and tatter
Of the undressed ghost but resolute
And bright in your own clothes,
Outstretched hands saying it is I.

But come and see, outside this room
The salvias still bloom, the window breathes
Warm air through rattan slats, in the French door
Shines the bronze haze of the crysanthemums,
Strange you are not reflected there.

Needing no space you are in me, light seeps
Down your sleeves, out of your shoes. Sit down,
Your glass is filled, have you seen Schubert?
I thought my heart tomb dark and cold
But love is rogue and it is I who call you.

Love Preparing to Fly
Gerard Manley Hopkins

He play'd his wings as though for flight;
They webb'd the sky with glassy light.
His body sway'd upon tiptoes,
Like a wind-perplexèd rose;
In eddies of the wind he went
At last up the blue element.

Journey's End
Padraig J Daly

After the tempests
And the lightning at sea,
I am ashore in a sunlit place.

I lift myself to climb the shingle
But my feet give way
And I crawl to the marram on my elbows.

I wait now,
Watching the white perfection of the gulls,
Until He welcomes me.

Acknowledgements

The editors and publisher thank all who supplied copyright permissions for work included in this collection. Every effort has been made to contact copyright holders; if, however, any infringement has inadvertently occurred we request the holders of such copyright to contact the publisher. For poems by W B Yeats permission granted by A P Watt on behalf of Michael B Yeats; by kind permission of the authors and The Gallery Press, Loughcrew, Oldcastle, County Meath, Ireland for 'Child Burial' and 'Elegy for a Child' by Paula Meehan from *The Man Who Was Marked By Winter* (1991), 'Stopping by a Clare Graveyard After Hours' by Michael Coady from *Oven Lane* (1987), 'Gravechild, Renvyle' by Eamon Grennan from *Wildly for Days* (1983), 'Be Still as You Are Beautiful' by Patrick MacDonogh from *Poems* (2001), 'In Memory of Patrick Boyle, 1905-1982' by Francis Harvey from *The Rainmakers* (1988), 'The Shell' by Brendan Kennelly from *The Voices* (1973); Paul Durcan for 'Going Home to Mayo, Winter, 1949'; Áine Miller for 'Caesura' and 'Hereafter'; Carcanet Press for 'Tree of Life' by Eavan Boland from *Boland Collected Poems*, 'Jill's Death' by George Buchanan from *Possible Being*; Frances Sommerville for 'The Grey Dusk' by Seumas O'Sullivan; Simon Campbell for poems by Joseph Campbell; Douglas Sealy for translation by Douglas Hyde; Patrick Walsh for poems by Michael Walsh; Thomas Kinsella for translations of 'Ag Críost an Síol' and 'An Phaidir Gheal' from *An Duanaire*; 'The Parting' © Sara Berkeley; Salmon Press for 'Where You Are' and 'Night Air' by Sheila O'Hagan from *The Troubled House* (1995), 'Ashes' and 'The Recipe' by Jean O'Brien from *The Shadow Keeper* (1997); Dedalus Press (www.dedaluspress.com) for poems by Robert Greacen, Conleth Ellis, John F Deane, Paul Murray, Enda Wyley, Padraig J Daly; The Random House Group for 'What Her Absence Means' and 'Lines of Leaving' from *Collected Poems* by Christy Brown, published by Secker & Warburg; the family of Winifred Letts; the estate of MJ MacManus; Bradshaw Books for 'The Left Shoe' by Mary Rose Callan from *The Mermaid's Head*; Faber and Faber Ltd for 'Mid-Term Break' and 'Valediction' by Seamus Heaney from *Death of a Naturalist*; David Higham Associates for 'Autobiography' and 'The Sunlight on the Garden' by Louis MacNeice; the five poems by Patrick Kavanagh from *Collected Poems*, edited by Antoinette Quinn (Allen Lane, 2004), by kind permission of the Trustees of the Estate of the late Katherine B Kavanagh through the Jonathan Williams Literary Agency.

Index of First Lines